"HOW TO BE A MAN"

Laura Martella

www.GentlemanNorman.com

To Randy,
you are a good Man!
Lets do lunch,
Love,
Norman

Published 2012, First Edition

Printed in the United States of America

Library of Congress Cataloging-in-Publication Data is available.

ISBN: 9 7 8 - 1 - 4 6 7 5 - 2 9 0 2 - 0

Author: Laura Martella

Consultant: Matt Benedict

Published by:

GN
GENTLEMAN
NORMAN.

Gentleman Norman, LLC
525 B Street, Suite 2200
San Diego, CA 92101
www.GentlemanNorman.com

In Loving Memory

Richard & Patricia Zweig

It is difficult to articulate the kind of people my parents were — solid, ethical, hard-working, neighborly people. They loved all animals and all of nature. Their connection with their dog Max and all of their grand-dogs, Walter, Norman and Howard, is still strong.

Max and Walter's ashes are buried with theirs in Winchester, Kentucky. I know they are all together in Heaven. Heaven wouldn't be Heaven without our dogs! My mom used to say, "Man just couldn't have invented a better companion than what God gave us in our doggies."

Here's to you, Mom & Dad. Thank you for all you instilled in me. I love you.

To My Birth Father

Bill Desmond

As a child of divorce, I consider myself fortunate to have grown up with two fathers and three sets of grandparents. I love you Daddy Bill.

Thank you for believing in me!

Before we get started ...

One VERY important thing I would
like you to know about me ...

As a man, I do have
BOUNDARIES!

I do NOT do silly costumes
and cutesy sunglasses or hats ...

I prefer golf shirts, cashmere sweaters
and the occasional jacket.

I've Discovered ...

It's Not so Bad Being the Little Guy

"BIG" is
an Attitude

Grooming and Wardrobe

Women Appreciate a

Well-Groomed Man

(Do Not Use Too Much Product. It is Not a Good Look!)

"REAL" Men
Wear Pink

Remember,

Cologne is Only for People

Who Get Close to You ...

Not Everyone on the Elevator!

There is Nothing Wrong
with a Man Bag ...

It's Practical

Remember the Importance

of a Breath Mint ...

Keep Them in Your Man Bag!

Relationship
Maintenance

At Some Point ...

Social Media is No Longer

"SOCIAL"

Women Like

EYE CONTACT

Regarding PDA (Public Display of Affection) ...

Sit as Close as Possible Without Being Inappropriate

"ACT"
Interested in
All that She Does ...

Fabric Swatches? ...

Why is she asking me?

NEVER

Answer the Question ...

" Does This Make My Butt Look Big? "

Let's Be Honest ...

There are Times When We Don't Know What to Say ...

Just Smile Adoringly …

Don't Ask ...

Just Smile Adoringly

When You Take Her Away For

a Romantic Weekend ...

Lets Talk About
Jewelry...

It's Simple ...

If You are Serious about Her ...

You are Going to Need a

Good Jeweler!

Every Man Needs a Jeweler on "Speed Dial"

Flowers...

And of Course, Every Man Needs a Florist on "Speed Dial"

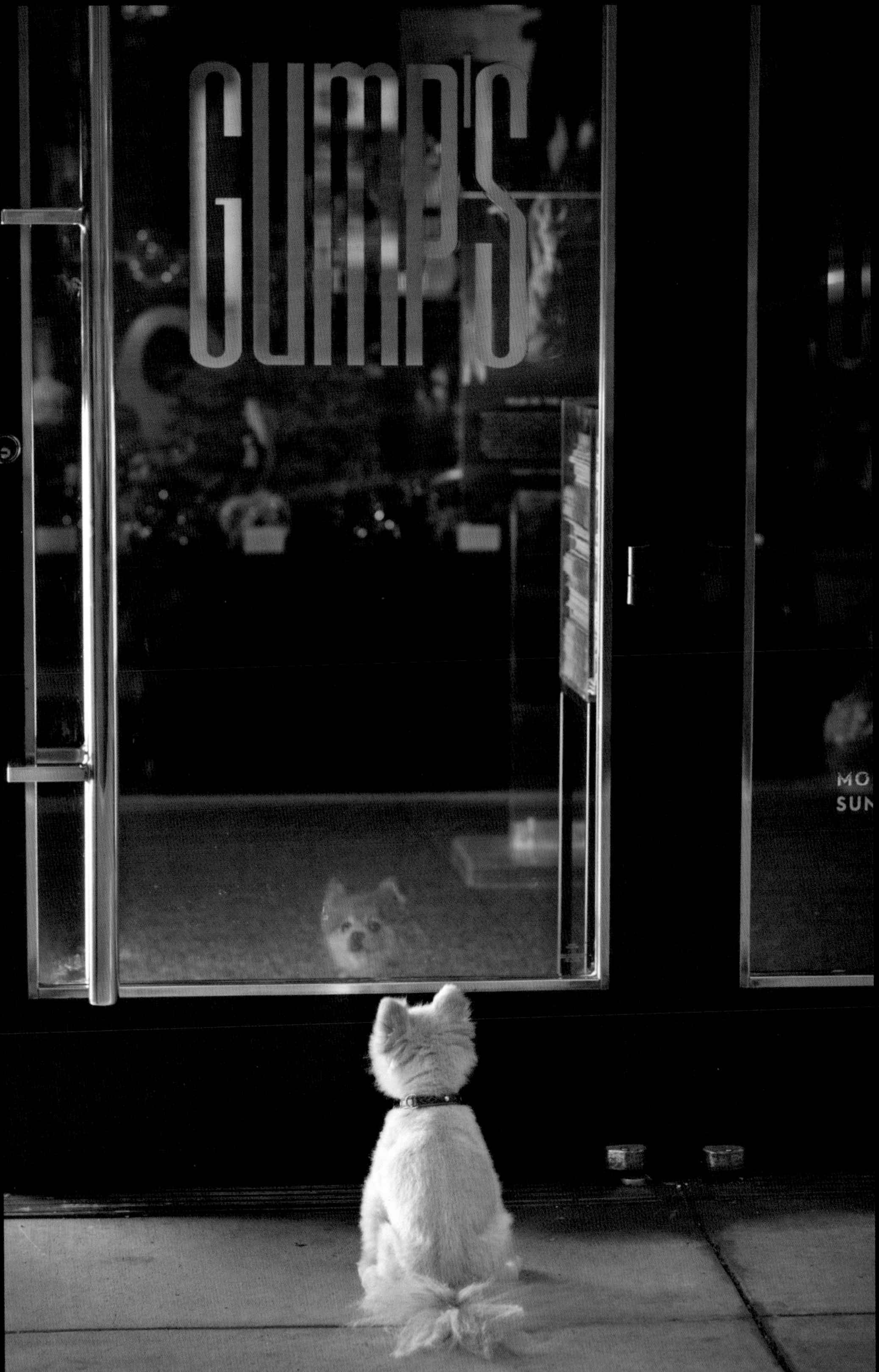
GUMP'S

For Your Sake....

Make Friends with Someone at Her Favorite Store

Repeat After Me:

I Love "Browsing," I Love "Browsing," I Love "Browsing"

GUMP'S

Go Ahead and Let Yourself Get Comfortable in the Stores ...
It's Really Not That Bad

Making the Best Out of an Afternoon of "Browsing"

Peacefully Waiting as
She Continues to "Browse"

Manners

Of Course It's Great
to "Hang" With the Guys ...

But When You're With Her,

Remember Your Table Manners

You May or May Not Be at the Head of the Table ...

... A Gentleman
Recognizes the Value
of Everyone on the Team

A Good Man
Always Remembers,
Always Respects
and Always Honors
Those Who Served

BIOGRAPHY BY JUDY MORGON

RALPH MORGON
WWII VETERAN

Ralph Morgon, a native Californian, was born in 1919; the 4th in a family of nine children.

When WWII began, Ralph was supervising Lockheed employees building airplanes. Even though he was married with an infant son, Ralph volunteered to join the Armed Services. His 6 brothers were already serving in the Navy, so when asked which branch he wanted to join, he immediately replied "Navy, of course!"

Ralph graduated from the aerial gunner's school at the Naval Air Station with honor grades and advanced from Seaman 1st class to Aviation Ordnanceman 3rd class. Afterward, he completed eight weeks of operational flight training and received his air crewman's wings. He served as a bombardier responsible for taking control of an airplane, guiding it to a bombing target, and then releasing the bomb load. During training he dropped more than 150 practice bombs, hitting each of his targets, and finishing top in his class.

After WWII Ralph returned to Lockheed but later decided to pursue a career as a fireman, just like his father. He is now a happily retired fire captain from the Pasadena Fire Department. Ralph has three children, three granddaughters, one great granddaughter, and two great grandsons on the way.

Remember to Take Care of the People

Who Take Care of You

Perhaps You Too

Will Become a VIP ...

It Really Impresses the Ladies

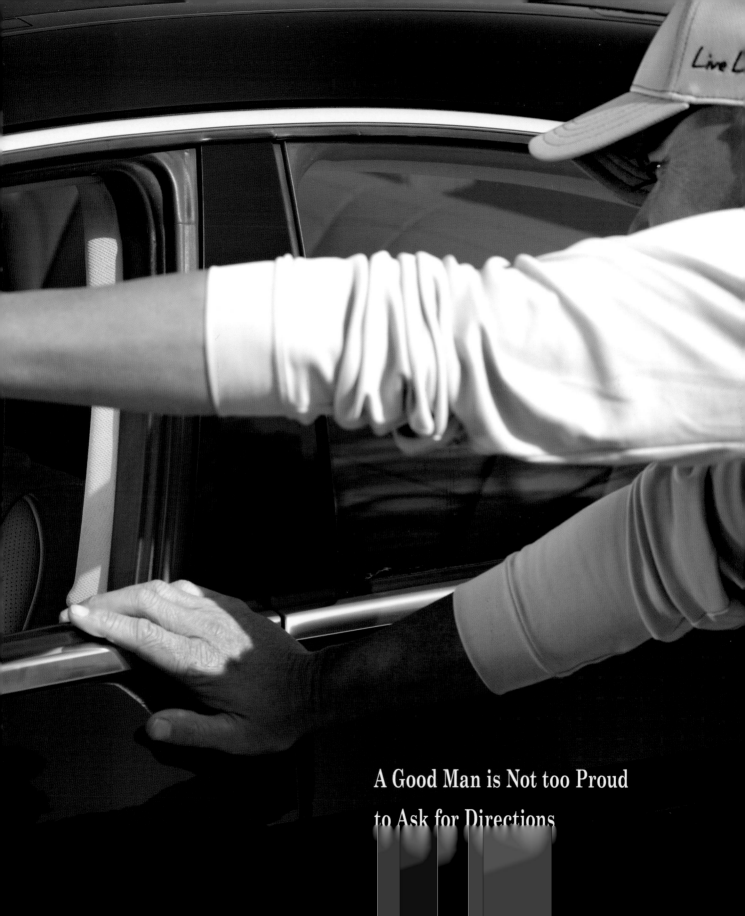

A Good Man is Not too Proud
to Ask for Directions

A Gentleman Always Sends

a Handwritten

"Thank You"

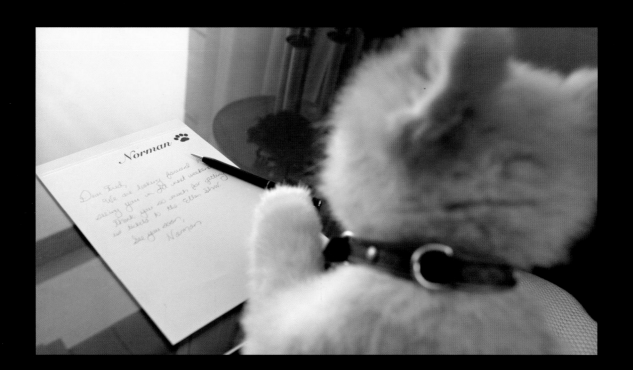

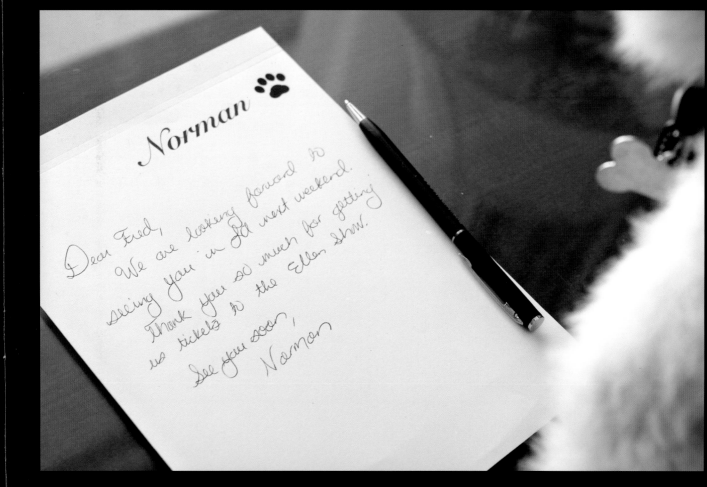

Norman

Dear Fred,
We are looking forward to
seeing you in SA next weekend.
Thank you so much for getting
us tickets to the Ellen Show.
See you soon,
Norman

You KNOW This One!

Difference of Opinion?

A Gentleman will Discuss it...

Face to Face ... Man to Man

We All Have Our Breaking Points ...

Go Ahead ...

Indulge in Some Downtime

Don't Ever Forget ...

Where You Came From

A Real Man Doesn't Need
to Feel Threatened by a
Younger Whipper-Snapper

I'm Quite Comfortable in
My Own Fur

Allow me to introduce my little brother,
Howard

Don't laugh, but Howard is 6 years old and still wears diapers ...
He went to "Doggy Rehab" for 4 weeks and
learned lots of cute tricks but not the potty training thing.
It's OK, I love Howard, he's my best friend.
He makes a lot of people happy.
As for the diaper, it just adds to his charm!

"Norman's Guide"

Finally a simple way to keep you
out of the "doghouse."

Download "Norman's Guide" from my website.
www.GentlemanNorman.com

It will simplify your life.
Spend a few minutes asking these questions,
I guarantee she will feel special
just because you asked.

Major Points! Trust me.

Norman's Guide

Your guide to keep you out of the "doghouse"

What is her Favorite Flower?
(What color? When is it in season?)
* Find a florist you like and put the number in your phone NOW.

What is her Favorite Chocolate?

What is her Favorite Perfume?

What is her Favorite Scented Candle?

(Don't forget to ask her where you can purchase)

Sizes You Need to Know:

Dress:	Blouse:
Robe:	Lingerie:
Shoe:	Ring:

What is her Favorite Spa? Body Products?

What is her Favorite Store?
(Ask if she has a sales person she likes to work with)

Good Luck
If you think of any other pertinent questions guys need to know—please share them with all of us.
Go to **www.GentlemanNorman.com**

What is her Favorite Wine / Champagne?

What is her Favorite Restaurant for Lunch / Dinner?

Favorite Local Hotel?

Favorite City?

Dream Vacation?

*Hint, Hint
* If you can't book her dream vacation just yet, a coffee table book about her favorite place is a thoughtful gesture.

* More hints to come...

Acknowledgements

I would like to thank my husband, *Michael*, for supporting my decision to do this book and for not ever taking any of "Norman's advice" personally. You are a true gentleman!

Thank you *Matt Benedict* for your guidance, participation and, most of all, not "cracking up" when I told you my idea for this book.

Thank you *Patricia Cross* for your ability to understand my vision and make it into a reality. You have the most wonderful sensitive heart, and it shows in your graphic design.

Thank you to my charming friend and attorney *John Cleary* at Procopio. Only you could make the legal aspects of this project fun. Also, thank you *Kathleen Pasulka-Brown* of Procopio for believing in Norman and for your expertise in publishing.

Thank you to all of our friends at **The Fairmont San Francisco**. Thank you *Mr. Klein* and *Mr. Wolfe* for the wonderful words you said about Norman in our video. I would also like to thank *Melissa Farrar, Mindi Morin* and *Michelle Gillman* for all of their help.

And of course, a well deserved thank you to all of my friends — for always listening and for having the decency to talk behind my back and not to my face!

Contributors:

Detour Salon
Brien Rea — Stylist
594 S. Coast Highway 101, Encinitas, CA 92024
760-634-1999
www.detoursalon.com

The Fairmont San Francisco
950 Mason Street, San Francisco, CA 94108
415-772-5000
www.fairmont.com/San Francisco

Robin Woolard Jewelers (Fairmont)
415-781-8107

Ornamento Flowers (Fairmont)
415-668-9624

Vendetta (Fairmont)
Men's Apparel & Vintage Cuban Cigars
415-397-7755

Gump's San Francisco
John Leafstedt — President
Carmen Roberson — Director of Marketing
135 Post Street, San Francisco, CA 94108
415-766-7628
www.gumps.com

The Inn at Rancho Santa Fe
5951 Linea Del Cielo
Rancho Santa Fe, CA 92067
858-756-1131
www.theinnatrsf.com

Rancho Santa Fe Golf Club
5827 Via de la Cumbre, Rancho Santa Fe, CA 92067
858-756-1182
www.rsfgolfclub.com

3rd Light Digital Media
2166 Hayes Street, Suite 300, San Francisco, CA 94117
415-221-5333
www.3rdlight.com

Photographer:

John Riedy — A very special heartfelt thanks to John Riedy, not only for your creativity and beautiful photography, but also for believing in "Gentleman Norman." There were moments when I thought we weren't getting "the shot," yet you always delivered!

John Riedy Photography
7691 Circulo Sequoia, Carlsbad, CA 92009
877-654-4271
www.johnriedy.com

Contributing Photographers:

Brianna Caster Photography
Brianna Caster — for your great energy.
714-658-1124
info@briannamariephotography.com
www.briannacaster.com

Coast Highway Photography
Kevin and Lenny — for all of the giggles!
415 S. Cedros Ave. #120, Solana Beach, CA 92075
858-350-4799
www.coasthighway.com

Bob Snell Photography
Bob Snell — for your experience and support.
6012 Paseo Delicias, Rancho Santa Fe, CA 92067
858-472-1113
www.bobsnell.com

Most of all — *Thank you to my "best friend" Norman.*
You are the most amazing spirit on the planet. I love you more than I could ever describe. I am so grateful to be your mom. The camera loves you, and you obviously love the camera too!
XOXO